The
WORST-CASE SCENARIO
POCKET GUIDE
RETIREMENT

By David Borgenicht &
Dan and Judy Ramsey

Illustrations by Brenda Brown

CHRONICLE BOOKS
SAN FRANCISCO

Copyright © 2009 by Quirk Productions, Inc.

Worst-Case Scenario® and The Worst-Case Scenario
Survival Handbook™ are trademarks of Quirk
Productions, Inc.

Library of Congress Cataloging in Publication Data
available.

ISBN: 978-0-8118-6837-2

Manufactured in China.
Designed by Jenny Kraemer
Illustrations by Brenda Brown
Visit www.worstcasescenarios.com

10 9 8 7 6 5 4 3 2 1

Chronicle Books LLC
680 Second Street
San Francisco, CA 94107
www.chroniclebooks.com

WARNING: You really should have been more careful. Now you're
facing one of the worst-case scenarios presented in this book—at least
you have the book with you, to refer to. But you must use your good
judgment and common sense and consult a professionally trained
expert to deal with these dangerous situations. The authors, publisher,
and experts disclaim any liability from any injury that may result
from the use, proper or improper, from the information contained
in this book. Nothing herein should be construed or interpreted to
infringe on the rights of other persons or to violate criminal statutes.
We urge you to be respectful and safe.

CONTENTS

INTRODUCTION

When we think about retirement, the images we hold in our heads are generally happy ones. We see ourselves sitting on the beach, golfing, fishing, playing bridge. We see ourselves taking up hobbies, volunteering, or finally starting that novel. We see ourselves traveling to exciting new places, visiting family regularly, and drinking cocktails with friends at increasingly early hours.

But as we've learned during more than a decade of researching and writing Worst-Case Scenario books, you just never know when things are going to take a sudden turn for the worse. While you can enjoy planning for pleasant dreams of retirement, you also need to be prepared for nightmares-come-true. Whether you're driving a golf cart in a hurricane or docking your yacht in a typhoon, spotting a card cheat or getting your child to move out of the house, this handy pocket guide is the required resource for a happy and safe result.

In the best worst-case tradition, we provide illustrated, step-by-step instructions on surviving these perils, and offer Instant Solutions to protect you against a variety of other threats. We also provide essential charts: the worst retirement locations, the worst places to take a nap, and things to use as a magnifying glass, among many others. And to fill those long, empty afternoons (and perhaps save your sanity or at least your marriage), there are lists— questions to ask your spouse and things that aren't as good as they used to be.

So congratulations on entering this new phase of life—and be on guard for a new set of dangers. You may have retired but danger and disaster have not.

—The Authors

The trouble with retirement
is that you never get a day off.
—Abe Lemons

BOARD ROOM TO BOREDOM

HOW TO TURN YOUR GARAGE INTO AN OFFICE

⭐ Have a garage sale.
Get rid of furniture, old clothes, sports equipment, toys, bicycles, antiques, and tools.

⭐ Move the grill, lawn mower, and gardening supplies into the shed.

⭐ Put up drywall.
Paint the walls beige.

⭐ Lay down carpet.
Install neutral-colored, wall-to-wall carpeting.

✪ Move in furniture.
Furnish your space with a desk, chairs, file
cabinets, bookcases, a conference table.

✪ Set up a computer.
Also equip your space with a printer,
photocopier, paper shredder, telephone,
and intercom system.

✪ Put IN and OUT boxes on your desk.
Hang a dry erase board and large wall
calendar. Stock your desk with pens,
pencils, highlighters, staples, paper clips,
notebooks, and manila folders.

✪ Install a water cooler and vending machine.
Move your coffee pot from your kitchen
to your new office.

✪ Hang curtains, motivational posters, and
your framed diploma on your wall.

Furnish the space with a desk, chairs, a file cabinet,
and a water cooler.

✪ Put pictures of your spouse, children, and grandchildren on your desk.

✪ Hang an Open/Closed sign on the door. Install a time clock at the doorway's entrance.

✪ Figure out what your business is.

THINGS THAT WERE BETTER AT THE OFFICE

- Gossip

- Coffee breaks

- Free pens/paperclips

- Free and fast Internet connection

- Younger coworkers

- Air conditioning

- Office parties

- Free phone

- Calling in sick

- Social network

- Professional network

- Mental exercise

- Regular paychecks

INSTANT SOLUTION

REMEDY A GROOMING MISHAP

Try a different style.

HOW TO FIND YOUR CONDO IN A CONDO DEVELOPMENT

⭐ Check the mailbox.
Open the box and look at the name on the bills and letters.

⭐ Ask people on the street.
Inquire at the management office. Ask neighbors for directions. Check with the mail carrier.

⭐ Study the driveways in your development.
Look for your car or other recognizable cars with identifying characteristics such as bumper stickers, roof racks, or flags. Locate your neighbor's fire-red Mustang convertible.

*Look for recognizable features such as flags,
lawn ornaments, or bumper stickers on your car.*

✪ Inspect the lawn.
Look for identifying lawn features such as garden gnomes, lawn jockeys, benches, or distinct flowers or shrubs.

✪ Use your garage door opener.
Roam the streets activating your remote garage door opener until it opens a garage door, which will most likely be yours.

How to Distinguish Your Condo from the Rest

✪ Paint your front door purple or orange.

✪ Place a skull-and-bones or other distinctive lawn flag in front of your place.

✪ Paint an arrow or hopscotch pattern on the sidewalk leading to your door.

✪ Put a nameplate with your last name on it beside your front door.

✪ Hang a grandchild's art work in your front window.

✪ Create a flower or vegetable garden in your front yard.

✪ Get a dog that will bark at the door until you return.

✪ Get a cat that will sit in the window.

WORST PLACES TO RETIRE

Too Expensive

Locations	Housing Costs
Birnam Wood, Montecito, California	$2–30 million
Field Point Circle, Greenwich, Connecticut	$1.4–25 million

Too Cold

Locations	Lowest Temperatures
International Falls, Minnesota	–40°F
Nome, Alaska	–54°F

Too Youth-Oriented

Locations	Annual Spring Breakers
Cancun, Mexico	More than 200,000
Fort Lauderdale, Florida	More than 20,000

HOW TO GET YOUR GROWN CHILD TO MOVE OUT

✪ | Do not cook her meals.

✪ | Do not do her laundry.

✪ | Do not pay her bills.

✪ | Raise the rent.
Inform your child that due to inflation and rising costs, your utility bills have increased and subsequently you have to raise rent.

✪ | Assign her household responsibilities.
Make her responsible for food shopping, cooking, yardwork, laundry, doing the dishes, and cleaning. Check and criticize her work.

Display suggestive affection for your mate
in front of your child.

⭐ Display suggestive affection for your mate in front of your child.
Act like you did when you first fell in love.

⭐ Invite your pastor to dinner often.

⭐ Talk openly about all the things you want to do when your child moves out.

⭐ Make noise when she is trying to sleep.

⭐ Ask where she is going and when she plans to return.
Repeat often.

⭐ Inquire about her love life often.
Ask specific, detailed questions.

✪ Take over her bedroom.
Tell her you need the space for your hobby. Transfer your model airplanes, coin collection, computer equipment, or scrapbooking supplies to her bedroom. Move her bedroom to the hot attic or unheated basement.

✪ Set a specific departure date.
Send a written eviction notice. Change the locks when the move-out date comes.

LEISURE FASHION MISTAKES

• Black dress socks and belt with sandals and shorts

• Outfit with more than three patterns

• Outfit with more than three colors

• Combining silk and tweed

• Shorts that are too short

• Pants that are too short (men)

• Pants that are too long

• Pants that sit too high

• Pants that fall too low

• T-shirts that are too short (men)

• Hats worn sideways or backwards

• Hats with chin straps

HOW TO INCORPORATE YOUR GRAND-CHILDREN INTO YOUR DAILY ACTIVITIES

⭐ Use them as golf caddies.
Divide the clubs equally among all the grandkids.

⭐ Ask them to be your ball boy or girl when playing tennis.
The smaller ones should work the net.

⭐ Go running with them.
Push a stroller while jogging for increased resistance. Have older children set your pace by riding their bikes beside you

while you are jogging. The bikes can carry drinking water, towels, or snacks.

✪ Let them play waiter/waitress.
Teach them how to serve and clear the table, open wine, and pour beverages. Let them dress up as a waiter or waitress when you entertain friends.

✪ Show them how to do the dishes.
The taller ones can put the dishes in the high cabinets.

✪ Let them set you up on the Internet.
Have your grandchildren teach you how to sell an item online, join a social networking site, or start a blog.

✪ Have them sort and roll your spare change.
Pay them a percentage of the value of the coins.

Use your grandchildren as golf caddies.

★ Show them how to garden.
Teach them to mow, weed, water, and plant.

★ Teach them to play card games.
Sharpen your bridge, poker, or rummy
skills by playing against your grandchildren.
Avoid War, Go Fish, or 52-Card Pick Up.

THINGS TO USE AS A
MAGNIFYING GLASS

- Glass jar

- Jeweler's loupe

- Glass paperweight

- Binoculars

- Two magnifying mirrors

THINGS THAT AREN'T AS GOOD AS THEY USED TO BE

- Today's youth
- Road conditions
- Customer service
- The weather
- Music
- Movies
- Dinner out
- Parties
- Television
- Newspapers
- Doctors' advice
- The taste of food
- Fuel prices
- Sex

HOW TO NAP AT A BORING COCKTAIL PARTY

1 Find a secluded location.
Choose an area where there are few party-goers. Close the blinds or drapes surreptitiously. Dim the lights.

2 Get in a comfortable position.
Select a chair, couch, bed, or other soft surface. Lie on your back or side. Avoid tipping your head so far back that you snore. Cover yourself with a jacket, sweater, or quilt.

3 Use a pillow.
Place a pillow or rolled up article of clothing under your head and neck for comfortable support. Put on sunglasses to hide your closed eyes. Insert ear plugs to reduce party noise.

Find a secluded location where there are few partygoers.

4 Relax.
Stretch your arms, tightening, then relaxing, the muscles. Repeat with your shoulders, torso, legs, and feet. Gently roll your head and neck. Relax facial muscles including your scalp, ears, and mouth.

5 Clear your mind.
Repeat a simple mantra, such as "omm," to clear the mind for relaxing. This will also discourage other guests from initiating conversation.

6 Limit your nap.
Set an alarm to wake you up after about 20 to 45 minutes.

How to Nap Anywhere

✪ In the park . . .
Select a desirable spot in the shade. Avoid areas with ant hills or dog poop. Clear any debris. Spread a blanket on the lawn.

✪ In the pool . . .

Wear a swimsuit or other light clothing.
Lather yourself with high SPF sunscreen.
Lay flat on a float with your legs dangling
into the water.

✪ On a bus, train, or plane . . .

Take off your jacket or request a blanket
to use as a pillow. Turn away from your
seatmate(s) to discourage conversation
and hide drooling. Put on sunglasses or an
eyeshade. Insert ear plugs or earphones.

Be Aware

- A power nap is a timed nap, typically for
  20 to 45 minutes, that terminates before
  a deep sleep or slow-wave sleep.
- A cat nap is for an undetermined time,
  often used as a break from activity.
- If you cannot fall asleep within 10 to 15
  minutes, simply rest. A power rest can
  be nearly as refreshing as a power nap.

Places NOT to Take a 4 p.m. Nap

- In the steam room
- At the grocery store
- In the car, while driving
- On the tennis court
- In the shower
- At a blackjack table
- On the ski slopes
- In a public restroom
- On the sidewalk
- At the bank
- On a surfboard
- At a carwash
- On a safari
- In the kitchen, while baking
- On the treadmill

INSTANT SOLUTION

MAKE A SHUFFLEBOARD COURT IN YOUR DRIVEWAY

*Use white duct tape to outline two facing triangles.
Number each section accordingly.*

QUESTIONS TO ASK YOUR SPOUSE

What do you want to do for dinner tonight?

Where should we take our next cruise?

Is it too early for a cocktail?

Do you want to go to the airport and people-watch?

What time should we nap today?

What friends would we invite on a round-the-world sailing trip?

Do you want to alphabetize the bookshelves with me?

Should we visit the kids today?

Do you want to play bocce or horseshoes?

Would you like me to wash your car again?

Do you think we would enjoy bird-watching?

What did we do yesterday?

THE DANGERS OF NAPPING

HOW TO TREAT SEA SICKNESS ON A CRUISE

★ Stay on deck.
Remain midship and watch the horizon.
Lie down on a deck chair in the fresh air.
Take deep breaths. Avoid the inside cabin
or small, enclosed spaces.

★ Ride the waves.
Sit straight and balance your upper body
over your hips as the boat moves.

★ Eat lightly.
Crackers and broth will settle your stomach.
Suck on hard candy.

★ Drink plenty of fluids. Avoid
alcoholic beverages.

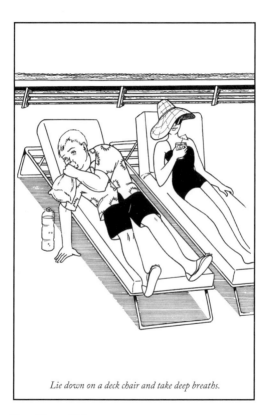

Lie down on a deck chair and take deep breaths.

✪ Take ginger or ginger supplements.

✪ Do not concentrate.
Do not look through binoculars for
an extended amount of time. Avoid
reading or staring at one point for a
prolonged period.

Be Aware
- Yawning, drowsiness, fatigue, and
  lethargy may be your first symptoms.
  Stomach upset and sweating usually
  follow. You may become pale, cold,
  and clammy. You may find it difficult
  to concentrate. Finally, nausea and
  vomiting commence.
- Wear an antimotion sickness wristband.
- Take motion sickness medicine an hour
  before you travel.

STRETCHING A DOLLAR
ON A FIXED INCOME

- Be a gracious dinner guest but don't reciprocate.

- Wear clothes once and return them for a refund.

- Cancel your newspaper subscription and read your neighbor's paper before he gets up in the morning.

- Dine at all-you-can-eat buffets and line your pockets with leftovers.

- Get free samples from cosmetic counters.

- Cancel cable and invite yourself to your children's houses to watch your favorite shows.

- Wash your car with the squeegee from the gas station.

- Dry and reuse paper towels.

- Stock up on free condiments from fast food restaurants.

HOW TO DRIVE AWAY CHATTY DINNER COMPANIONS

✪ Pretend to be hard of hearing.
Shout "What?" each time a tablemate
addresses you. Then respond inappropriately
to each comment or question.

✪ Act cold and aloof.
Literally hold your head high and look down
your nose at everyone.

✪ Act ill.
Cough often and loudly. Scratch vigorously.
Sneeze frequently.

Act ill by coughing, sneezing, and scratching.

⭐ Be obnoxious.
Deliberately turn away from anyone who addresses you. Focus only on your favorite dinner companion.

⭐ Criticize the food.
Make derogatory comments about what everyone else has ordered. Compare the way the food looks to unpleasant objects.

⭐ Remain silent.
Do not speak at any time during the dinner. Order from the menu by pointing and grunting. Feign incomprehension at any attempt to engage in conversation. Enjoy your meal.

RETIREMENT AGES AT WHICH SOCIAL SECURITY BENEFITS KICK IN

Born	Age
1937 or earlier	65 years
1938	65 and 2 months
1939	65 and 4 months
1940	65 and 6 months
1941	65 and 8 months
1942	65 and 10 months
1943–1954	66 years
1955	66 and 2 months
1956	66 and 4 months
1957	66 and 6 months
1958	66 and 8 months
1959	66 and 10 months
1960 and later	67 years

HOW TO TREAT SUNBURN

⭐ Move to a shaded or indoor location.
Already-burned skin can still continue
to burn if exposure to the sun continues.

⭐ Take a cool shower.
Avoid extreme hot or cold showers. Adjust
the shower head to reduce water pressure.

⭐ Submerge yourself in an oatmeal bath.

⭐ Place cool, damp cloths over the burn.
Replace damp cloths as they absorb heat.

⭐ Apply aloe vera.
Rub your skin liberally with aloe vera gel.

⭐ Place wet, caffeinated teabags on the burn area.
Tannins contained in tea cool and
soothe skin.

Place cool, damp cloths and wet, caffeinated teabags on burn area.

✪ Stay hydrated.
Drink plenty of water. Avoid alcohol.

✪ Wear loose-fitting clothing.
Cotton or linen is best.

✪ Take anti-inflammatory medication.
Ibuprofen will help ease the pain.

✪ Stay out of the sun.
Occupy yourself with indoor activities.

Be Aware

- Never apply ice to a sunburn as it can further damage skin cells.
- Do not use petroleum jelly as it holds in heat.
- Check your medication warnings. Many medications are heightened by sun exposure.
- Always use a high SPF, even on cloudy days.

INSTANT SOLUTION

SURVIVE A NORWALK VIRUS OUTBREAK

Barricade door

Open porthole

Avoid contact with food, water, and people to protect yourself from the gastrointestinal virus.

SPORTS THAT RESULT IN THE MOST INJURIES FOR RETIRED PEOPLE

1. Cycling

2. Aerobics/Weightlifting

3. Snow Skiing

4. Golf

5. Fishing

6. Tennis

7. Swimming/Diving

8. Bowling

9. Skating

10. Baseball/Softball

HOW TO TREAT ROAD RASH

1 Remove any clothing from around the wound.
Skidding when you fall off your bike will partially tear your clothing. Cut away or remove the rest.

2 Clean out debris.
Using sterile gauze, carefully brush away any debris, such as cloth, glass, gravel, leaves, or dirt that has gotten in the abrasion. Avoid scrubbing or rubbing, which can further irritate the wound.

3 Trim away dead skin.
Use sterile medical scissors to cut away any loose skin.

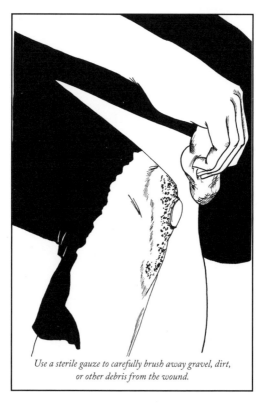

Use a sterile gauze to carefully brush away gravel, dirt,
or other debris from the wound.

4 | Irrigate with saline.
Flush out the wound with soap and warm water or a mild saline solution.

5 | Apply a topical antibiotic ointment.
Cover the wound.
Choose a dressing that won't stick to the abrasion, such as gauze with petroleum jelly. Avoid plain gauze. Secure with medical tape.

6 | Lift bandage daily.
Allow the wound to breathe and fluids to drain.

7 | Change dressing often.
Clean wound daily with soap and water. Reapply ointment and cover with new gauze.

8 | Watch for signs of infection.
Redness, pus, fever, or a foul smell can all be signs of infection.

Be Aware

- Bike accidents are the most common cause of road rash. Wear protective clothing, especially if you are traveling at high speeds, and leathers if you're on a motorcycle.
- Avoid undiluted antiseptics, which can actually harm the tissue under the skin, delaying the healing process.
- Verify when you had your last tetanus shot. Road rash can make you susceptible to tetanus, an infectious disease that can develop in burn-like abrasions.
- Once healed, the area will be susceptible to sunburn. Apply a high SPF and keep covered when outside.

HOW TO TREAT A KNITTING NEEDLE INJURY

1 Stand up slowly.
Avoid bumping or otherwise disturbing the needle.

2 Feel for the needle at the entry point.
If you cannot reach the entry point, ask a spouse, child, or other companion to assist you.

3 Remove the needle.
Carefully pull the needle from the wound in one swift motion.

4 Stop the bleeding.
Apply pressure with a clean cloth, piece of fabric, or knitted garment.

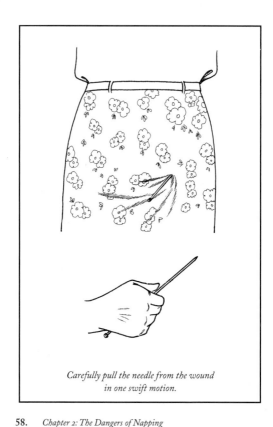

*Carefully pull the needle from the wound
in one swift motion.*

5 Disinfect the wound.
Wash the wound in a solution of one part warm water to one part hydrogen peroxide. Apply an antibiotic ointment.

6 Cover the wound with a sterile bandage. Secure with medical tape.

7 Watch the wound for signs of infection.

Spice Up Activities

Before	After
Poker	Strip poker
Daily walks in the park	Bungee jumping
Afternoon tea	Happy hour
Synchronized swimming	Skinny dipping
Work on train set	Train hop
Volunteer at library	Volunteer at adult bookstore
Cocktail party	Beer pong
Croquet	Paintball
Hiking	Rock climbing
Read romance	Read erotica
Build model plane	Take flying lessons
Watch TV quiz shows	Try out for TV quiz shows
Visit hairdresser	Get complete makeover
Discuss politics	Run for local office

HOW TO PREVENT SNORING

★ Change sleep positions.
Snoring is often caused by lying on your back. Train yourself to sleep on your side or stomach.

★ Sew a tennis ball to the back of your pajamas.
Prevent yourself from turning over onto your back in the middle of the night by attaching a tennis ball to your back. This will force you to lie on your side, effectively ridding you of the habit.

★ Avoid alcohol.
Alcohol and other sedatives increase muscle relaxation, which increases snoring.

★ Change your diet.
Reduce the amount of refined carbohydrates

and dairy products that you consume. Both increase mucus production which can cause snoring. Also avoid eating large meals at night right before bed.

⭐ Exercise.
Extra body fat, especially bulky neck tissue, can cause snoring. Losing just 10 percent of your body weight can improve your overall breathing.

⭐ Apply nasal strips.
Open nasal passages with adhesive nose strips.

⭐ Use a throat spray.
Lubricate your throat with a spray that will relax the throat muscles.

⭐ Practice aromatherapy.
Reduce nasal congestion with essential oils. Leave a jar of majoram oil open on your nightstand while you sleep. Add a

Sew a tennis ball to the back of your pajamas.

few drops of eucalyptus oil to a water-filled humidifier. Breathe in the steam just prior to going to bed.

⭐ Use a neti pot.
Reduce allergens in your sinuses by washing out your nasal passages with a neti pot. Fill the pot with water and ¼ teaspoon of salt. Hold your head over a sink at an angle so your chin is parallel with your forehead. Tilt the pot so the tip of the arm enters one nostril. Allow the water to flow in one nostril and out the other. Repeat in the other nostril.

⭐ Prop up your mattress.
Put a dictionary, encyclopedia, or phone book under your mattress to raise your head and change the angle of your neck.

INSTANT SOLUTION

PUT OUT A GRILL FIRE

Smother a fire on a charcoal grill by covering the fire liberally with baking soda or flour.

CHAPTER 3
HOBBIES

"WHAT DO YOU DO ALL DAY?"

HOW TO SPOT A CARD CHEAT

⭐ Examine the cards.

Before play begins, look for irregularities in the cards that might help a cheater identify a particular card. Marks in a round design, like marks on a clock face, may indicate the value of a card; an ace is marked at one o'clock, an eight at eight o'clock. Nicks, nail marks, stains, and crimps may also be marks. Beware if a player bends cards during play.

⭐ Watch for false shuffling.

Confirm that the dealer actually shuffles the deck; a cheat may have brought in a prestacked deck. An overhand shuffle can stack a deck right in front of your eyes. Insist on a reshuffle if you are suspicious. Require that the deck be cut by someone other than the dealer.

Watch the
dealer shuffle

Watch for facial expressions, body language, or other
nonverbal cues that can be used to signal another player.

★ Watch for team cheating.
Shufflers who first bend the deck can be sending a signal to the cutter where to cut the deck; the bent half of the deck should be easy to spot when the deck is placed on the table for the cutter. A cheater can also leave a slight jog in the deck indicating to the accomplice where to make the cut.

★ Listen for verbal cues between partners.
Repeated phrases may have hidden meanings. Be suspicious of players (or nonplayers) who wander the room, then interact with another player. Signals can also include nonverbal cues such as facial expressions, body language, gestures, and subtle indicators such as sighs or sneezes.

★ Watch the banker.
Keep an eye on the tender of the pot, the banker, or other special task holders. Cheaters can palm a chip when distributing winnings, skim off bank winnings, short

change a player, or otherwise sweeten their own winnings.

Be Aware

- Mirrors, windows, and even eyeglasses (especially reflective sunglasses) can reflect a player's hand.
- Draw cards to determine who sits where to decrease cooperative cheating.
- Make a rule that someone other than the dealer shuffles the cards.
- The deck should sit squarely on the table. An even slightly spread deck can reveal marks to a cheater.
- Require that players keep cards on the table at all times.
- Do not be fooled by a good hand; a cheat may deal you a good hand, but his will be better.
- Use a position or joker on the bottom of the deck so that no one can see the bottom card and the dealer cannot deal from the bottom of the deck.

Instant Solution

Blend in with the Locals
When Traveling

Do not dress like a tourist.

HOW TO TAKE LEFTOVERS FROM THE BUFFET

1 Bring containers.
Take along small plastic containers with tightly locking lids or zippered plastic bags. Carry the containers in a lined backpack for easy transport.

2 Find an isolated table.
Select a table away from the buffet line, kitchen, and other diners. Place your backpack on the seat next to you and away from the view of others, especially servers.

3 Act casual.
Keep a low profile. Do not draw attention to yourself or your actions.

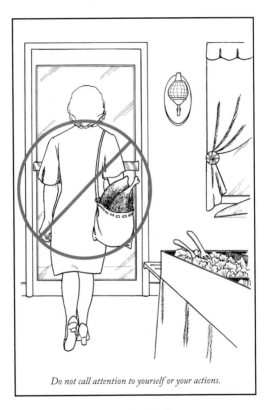

Do not call attention to yourself or your actions.

4 Choose transportable foods.
Stroll through the buffet line selecting
your meal as well as your leftovers. Select
foods without liquids, such as fried
chicken, baked potatoes, or bread. Avoid
foods such as soup, baked beans, dips,
and ice cream.

5 Take the food to your table.

6 Transfer food to containers.
Move food from your plate to your
containers when no one is paying attention.
Use a napkin ostensibly to wipe your mouth
but then also cover your movement of
food from plate to container. Secure lids
tightly and zip bags closed. Slide the
containers into your backpack on the seat
next to you. Continue eating your meal.

7   Make another trip to the buffet table. Add food to your plate. Do not leave your old plate on the table as a server may come to clear it and notice your activities.

8   Add more food to the containers.

9   Repeat trips to the buffet table and filling containers.

10   Exit quietly.
Leave food on your plate, and a generous tip.

Be Aware

- Choose a busy, successful buffet. Visit the restaurant in advance to assess the scene and plan your strategy.
- If you get caught, explain that you were just taking the leftovers.

CLEVER WAYS TO TAKE YOUR MEDICINE

- Hide medicine in a mixed drink, such as an Old Russian (Ensure and Kahlua) or a 5 A.M. Sunrise (Metamucil and Tequila).

- Grind your meds and add them to your mashed potatoes. Pour on gravy to mask the flavor.

- Alternate each pill with an M&M or a spice drop.

- Put pills in with a bowl of cereal.

- Replace the chocolate chips in an already baked cookie with your pills.

- Mix pills in with trail mix or mixed nuts.

- Hold your nose, pop in the pill(s), and swallow quickly. Chase with water.

HOW TO DRIVE A GOLF CART IN A HURRICANE

⭐ Remove roof top.
High wind speeds can easily blow off the roof top, posing a danger to you and your passengers.

⭐ Seek firm ground.
Avoid puddles, running water, swampy areas, or uncertain terrain.

⭐ Steer clear of fallen or falling trees.

⭐ Shift weight to rear wheels.
Move your golf bags and passenger above the rear wheels to improve traction. Move as far back in the driver's seat as you can.

Step out of the cart and press the gas pedal with your hand.

✪ Reduce cart weight.
If the cart is sinking or not gaining traction, jettison golf bags and ask passengers to walk. Step out of the cart and press the gas pedal with your hand.

✪ Increase traction under wheels.
Place small rocks, a golf towel, or articles of clothing under wheels for additional traction.

✪ Seek shelter.
Move to an indoor location as soon as possible. High winds can easily roll your cart or blow trees or other objects into your path.

Be Aware

- Most hurricane fatalities are a result of inland flooding. Move inland as much as possible and avoid water. Do not attempt to cross flowing water. The average person can be swept off their feet in just six inches of flowing water.

INSTANT SOLUTION

CUSTOMIZE YOUR GOLF CART

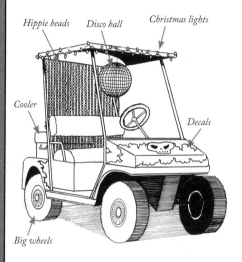

Hippie beads

Disco ball

Christmas lights

Cooler

Decals

Big wheels

Decorate your cart according to your style.

HOW TO SAIL THROUGH A TYPHOON

1   Reduce speed.

2   Determine your position.
Plot your position on your chart relative
to the position of the storm, wind direc-
tion and speed, and estimated time to
your destination.

3   Adjust your course.
Navigate towards the closest shoreline.

4   Instruct all passengers to put on their
personal flotation devices immediately.
Put on your life jacket as well.

5   Assign specific duties to each passenger.
Instruct one crew member to look out for

danger areas, debris, or other boats, and
another to turn on all bilge pumps.

6 Close hatches, ports, and windows.

7 Secure loose items.
Move loose items below deck. Tie down
anything that cannot be moved below deck.

8 Lower the sails or change to storm sails.

9 Prepare life boat.
Equip with emergency food, water, and
first aid kit.

10 Unplug any electrical equipment.
Turn off circuit breakers and disconnect
antennas. Instruct passengers and crew to
avoid contact with metal objects.

11 Direct the bow into winds.
Approach waves at a 40- to 45-degree angle.

Tie down anything that cannot be moved below deck.

12 Keep passengers low and to the center of the boat.

Rig jack lines, life lines, and safety harnesses to anyone that needs to be on deck.

Be Aware

- Clouds are the best indicators of weather. Watch for stratus clouds that lower or cumulus clouds that rise up and turn into cumulonimbus clouds, both indicators of approaching storms.
- When you first realize you are facing inclement weather, radio in to the Coast Guard, as well as other boats. Inform them of your location and float plan.
- There are three main distress calls on the VHF radio:

    Mayday: Grave and imminent danger to life or vessel (fire, person overboard, etc.)

    Pan-pan: Help needed (less severe than Mayday)

    Securite: Hazards to navigation.

LABOR-EXPANDING TIPS TO FILL YOUR DAY

In the Kitchen	In the Backyard	In the Basement
Grind your own coffee beans by hand.	Start a compost pile.	Label and scrapbook all photographs.
Squeeze oranges for fresh orange juice.	Mow crop circles.	Reorganize all your books by genre or color.
Make home-made spaghetti sauce.	Build a patio.	Construct a wine cellar.
Brew your own beer.	Practice topiary.	Paint a mural.

HOW TO GET YOUR JOB BACK

★ Schedule a casual lunch with your former boss to "catch up."

★ Sell yourself.
Present your former boss with a list or reasons why you should be rehired: you are experienced, you work well with other employees, you have many industry contacts. Mention that hiring you back will eliminate the need for training a young, inexperienced worker. Remind him that you were a hard worker; refer to specific accomplishments, awards, or achievements.

★ Bargain.
Offer to work part-time or to job share without health benefits.

⭐ Grovel.
Show your former boss pictures of your wife, children, and pets. Explain their needs.

⭐ Offer a bribe.
Promise your former boss use of your boat for long weekends, expense paid trips, or a cash payment.

⭐ Threaten.
Casually mention your familiarity with antiage discrimination laws.

⭐ Compromise.
If your old job is not available, offer to work an entry-level position for a while to prove your dedication. Work on call or fill in for vacations and sick leave.

Take an entry-level job to show you're willing to work.

INDEX

ACKNOWLEDGMENTS

David Borgenicht would like to thank Sarah O'Brien, Jay Schaefer, Steve Mockus, Brianna Smith, Jenny Kraemer, and Brenda Brown for making this book happen—and he'd like to invite you all to stay with him at his condo in Boca someday in about twenty-five years.

ABOUT THE AUTHORS

David Borgenicht is the creator and coauthor of all the books in the Worst-Case Scenario series, and is president and publisher of Quirk Books (www.quirkbooks.com). He is nowhere near retirement age, but he nevertheless enjoys a good early bird special. He lives in Philadelphia.

Dan Ramsey is pre-tired. At 63, he's not ready to give up writing just yet—he's authored 91 books! However, the thought of retirement gains appeal daily and he's already making serious plans. He and his child-bride, **Judy Ramsey**, extensively researched the worst-case scenarios for retirement and report their findings in this book of truths. The Ramseys live in Northern California in a wandering trailer. They also operate FixItClub.com.

Brenda Brown is an illustrator and cartoonist whose work has been published in many books and publications, including the Worst-Case Scenario series, *Esquire*, *Reader's Digest*, *USA Weekend*, *21st Century Science & Technology*, the *Saturday Evening Post*, and the *National Enquirer*. Her Web site is www.webtoon.com.

MORE WORST-CASE SCENARIO PRODUCTS

VISIT OUR PARTNERS' WEBSITES FOR MORE WORST-CASE SCENARIO PRODUCTS:

- ✪ Board games
  www.universitygames.com
- ✪ Gadgets
  www.protocoldesign.com
- ✪ Mobile
  www.namcogames.com
- ✪ Posters and puzzles
  www.aquariusimages.com/wcs.html

For updates, new scenarios, and more, visit:
www.worstcasescenarios.com

To order books visit:
www.chroniclebooks.com/worstcase

MORE WORST-CASE SCENARIOS

HANDBOOKS

- The Worst-Case Scenario Survival Handbook
- Travel
- Dating & Sex
- Golf
- Holidays
- Work
- College
- Weddings
- Parenting
- Extreme Edition
- Life

ALMANACS

- History
- Great Outdoors
- Politics

CALENDARS

- Daily Survival Calendar
- Daily Survival Calendar: Golf

POCKET GUIDES

- Dogs
- Breakups
- Retirement
- New York City